FIT FOR BUSINESS

Discover the 9 **key** mistakes costing **your business** time, money & customers and learn how to **overcome** them

Contents

Introduction

Do you find yourself with less and less free time? Undercharging for your time and expertise? Clueless about how to attract more of the right type of customer?

In this book you will discover some of the most common mistakes made in business that are costing you time, money and customers. You will also learn some simple yet effective techniques to help you combat these mistakes.

Emma Melhuish

This book has been written to provide you with a resource that can be used time and time again. I wanted you to be able to read it from cover to cover and be inspired to take action in order to achieve your goals.

Each section gives you a short, no-nonsense account of the common mistake and a number of simple solutions, author's tips and resources to help you to take immediate action to move your business forward.

Reading this book is certainly not designed to give you all the answers but it is intended to open your mind to other experiences and force you to ask questions of yourself and your business. Treat this book like a workbook. Highlight key points, take notes and most importantly take action on the ideas you generate from reading it.

On to mistake number one...

 The books you don't read won't help."
– Jim Rohn

Why the way you think impacts **massively** *on your results*

Many people have heard of the 80/20 rule, or the Pareto Principle, which states that 20 percent of any effort will usually provide 80 percent of the results. Leadership and peak performance expert, Anthony Robbins, has also applied the 80/20 rule to the study of success. He states that in almost every circumstance:

80 percent of success is due to psychology, mindset, beliefs, and emotions and only 20 percent is due to strategy. The specific steps needed to accomplish a result."

Typically, people in the early stages of their business wish to improve or ensure the success of their efforts. They first think of learning to write a business plan, managing an inventory, creating a balance sheet, establishing or improving sales systems and building a marketing platform. Although these skills and strategies are essential, the rule suggests that they only form 20 percent of what is necessary to achieve results. Therefore, without the other 80 percent, and without the proper psychology in place, strategy will be of very limited use.

To be successful at anything that you do, you must have the correct mindset. This applies in business as in any other area of our lives. In fact, it probably applies more in business, simply because in business you are largely responsible for your own success. To become successful in business, you need more than a killer product, a plan, or a market. You need the ability to see opportunities, to be creative, innovative, to overcome fears, and you need the willingness and persistence to turn ideas in your head into physical reality.

If you are having any limiting beliefs about whether or not you are worthy of success, or if you feel nothing good ever happens for you, then you will not be able to have that long-term success that you truly desire and deserve. You might have success for a short time but when those limiting beliefs start creeping back, your success will start to dwindle away. It is when you believe in yourself and know that you are worthy of success, in addition to taking the necessary steps to grow your business, that you are telling a different story - a story of success.

The right mindset is critical for long-term business success. Running a business takes a lot of work. If you are not prepared to put in the work, your chances of success will be very low. The obvious question is, therefore, what is the right mindset for business?

The crucial skill necessary for long-term success in your business is the ability to keep yourself motivated. This represents the key difference between being employed and running your own business. When you run your own business, you need to ensure that you are self-motivated and that, even when things are not going fantastically well, you can still jump out of bed each morning and run your business to the best of your ability. If you are not able to keep yourself motivated, you will have real challenges in being in control of your own business.

Another important mindset that you must master is persistence. Unlike being in a job, there is not going to be anybody breathing down your neck each day making sure that you are on top of things. Doing something a few times, then giving up because you did not get the results that you expected is just not enough. You need be persistent with your business activity day after day, after day. If you have the mindset of a person who gives up at the first hurdle, you will struggle to succeed in business.

If you think about the mindset of an entrepreneur (and to be truly successful in business this is the way you need to think), they are innovators and inventors – they are able to visualise what does not yet exist with complete clarity. They have the passion to drive themselves forward and create their ideas, holding their purpose even in the face of adversity. Most importantly, they have the correct mindset which allows them to revise and improvise, to constantly learn and look for ways to adapt to new conditions and circumstances; and they have the courage to take risks, believing ultimately in their own success and the success of their businesses.

Strategy is important too — it will lead you to the accomplishment of the vision. However, vision, passion and a positive mindset are necessary to guide strategy. Without these elements in place, no killer product, perfect business plan or sizeable target market will guarantee that your business will thrive and grow.

 With the right vision, passion, and mindset, your chances of success are exponentially greater, no matter what the business climate." - Anthony Robbins

The entrepreneurial mindset is composed of the following three elements:

Belief

Successful entrepreneurs believe in themselves, in their businesses, and in their products or services. They also believe in their ability to succeed and they understand the power of beliefs to determine what they will or will not do, what they will or will not notice, and the actions that they will or will not take.

Attitude

Entrepreneurship requires specific emotional and mental traits that can be grouped under the term attitude. The attitudes that people bring to work will determine whether or not they are suited to entrepreneurship. According to research, the specific attitudes that the most successful entrepreneurs share include courage, persistence, adaptability, curiosity, collaboration, future focus, self-fulfillment, the desire to learn, and the willingness to take action.

Focus

If there is one key trait of a successful entrepreneurial mindset, it is the ability to direct one's focus; to put time, energy, and attention towards what will help to build the business and mitigate whatever will hold it back.

Successful entrepreneurs focus on three things. Firstly, they look for opportunities where others see only obstacles. Secondly, they are able to focus with laser-like precision on the goal at which they are aiming, not letting the negative advice of others deter them. Thirdly, they manage risk and overcome fear by controlling their focus. Almost every study of the entrepreneurial mindset cites the ability to manage risk as a key to success.

Here are some specific things you can do to ensure that you develop the business mindset of an entrepreneur:

1. Understand that the purpose of business is to make money. You must determine whether your business is a business that requires a higher level of development, in order to acquire a higher level of income, or a hobby which makes you a little extra money.

2. Be strategic about your business activity. Do not attend just any networking event, training, or take on any job; know what you want the outcomes of these activities to be before you invest any time and/or money in them. Before I commit to attending any training or event I always do my research. If I decide it

is worthwhile attending, I ensure I have a specific outcome in mind. For example at a training event I once attending my objective was to make everyone aware of my business and to forge a relationship with the organisation running the training. As a result I came away from that training not only with an abundance of new skills, but also a new coaching client and a speaking slot for the training hosts. Take the time to consider the REAL cost - money, time, childcare, food, travel and accommodation before you attend any training or networking event. In order to recoup your investment, your reasons for investing in the training must be something in addition to meeting people and wanting to learn something new. It is obvious that you will meet people at a networking event and you will learn something during a training day. Therefore, your purpose for attending any event must be both aligned with your vision and focused on profitability. Make sure that you have a specific outcome in mind before investing in business activities like networking and training.

3. Ensure that you connect with your business profitability. Know your profit margin, cash flow, competitive advantage, sales goals, and your key profit indicators. If you can already answer these, you are well on your way to having a business mindset. Some great resources that I recommended are: Understanding Business Accounting For Dummies by John A. Tracy CPA and Colin Barrow; Double Your Business: How to Break Through

the Barriers to Higher Growth, Turnover and Profit by Lee Duncan; Beyond Performance: How Great Organizations Build Ultimate Competitive Advantage by Scott Keller and Colin Price; Toolbox - Essential Selling Skills To Win More Business by Phil M Jones and my favourite is an online accounting software called xero.com.

4. Understand your business strategy and ensure you implement it into your daily activities. It is very easy to become caught up on menial day-to-day tasks which may not be moving your business forward. Focus on the end goal and plan in detail all the steps you need to get there. Whenever you start something new, ask yourself the question: "Is this task moving me towards my end goal?" If the answer is "No", stop doing it immediately and move onto something that is in line with your business strategy.

5. Be open to multiple streams of income and multiple business opportunities. I met a lady at a conference recently, and I will never forget what she said: "I have one business that is my passion, it makes me a good income and I run it myself. I have another business that generates substantial profit for me and someone else runs it on my behalf." My point: Do not put all your eggs in one basket - this is part of having a business mindset.

6. Understand the emotional ties that you have to your business. By understanding these, you will break through any personal barriers that prevent you from doing what you say you are going to do and doing what you want to do. The next time you get emotional in your business, jot down how you are feeling and what has triggered it. This is how you begin to acknowledge which emotions are stopping you from doing good business.

7. Be social, even if you do not feel like it. Shutting yourself away from everyone is a common mistake too many business owners make when times are tough. If your business seems to have slowed down, attend more networking events and raise awareness of your business through social networks and social media sites (remember you can get someone else to help with this). If you do not have one already, you may want to consider creating a mastermind group of people with whom you can consult about business challenges.

8. Avoid negative people and take care with what you feed your mind. It is easy to start and end your day watching the news, but beware of the negative messages from the headlines. Instead, read something inspiring, ideally just before bed and when you first wake up. The last thing you put into your mind before you go to sleep should be positive and inspiring because that is what your subconscious mind will focus on

during your sleep. In addition, think about the people you spend the most time with, do they push you forward or hold you back? Jim Rohn once said: "You are the average of the five people you spend the most time with." For me this quote is extremely powerful and one that I remind myself of over and over again. Understand that others around you can determine how you think, act and, ultimately, how successful you will be.

9. Get up and move more! Exercise is one of the first things that people skip when under pressure. When we are feeling stressed, our body produces noradrenalin, a stress hormone that can affect our attention and quality of thinking. Exercise releases endorphins and these counter the build-up of stress hormones in the body. Your brain functions better if you exercise. This does not mean that you have to join a gym; it is easy to find ways to incorporate exercise into your day. Take a few flights of stairs instead of the lift, or simply go for a walk to get your blood pumping and help to clear your mind.

The number one reason why most people fail

 What your mind can conceive and believe, it can achieve."
- Napoleon Hill

Often referred to as "limiting beliefs" if these are not addressed and understood they can prevent you from getting your new business off the ground, growing your business to new levels, and/or attracting wealth.

Let me put this in context...

It is our personal viewpoints or 'belief systems' that provide us with an essential base of principles and rules that drive the way we think, feel and behave. These viewpoints are created out of a need to store and organise life experiences in a way that makes sense and helps us to understand the world in which we live. We are constantly inundated with new information and, to make this easier to process; we compare and match up this new information with our previous experiences. This previously stored information, grouped with the new information, combines to create our personal belief systems.

There are two main types of belief system:

The first belief system is formed by common sense and repetition. Here the person does not have any real desire to believe it, other than the desire to make sense of the world. For example, the earth is a sphere, gravity is a pulling force that keeps us on the ground; breaking a bone hurts.

The second belief is formed out of the need to protect oneself, either psychologically or emotionally from perceived threat or fear. For example, "money is evil", "sales people are scammers", "I don't have the skills to do that."

Now if I were to ask you which of the two main beliefs are most damaging to your business what would you say? You would be right to say the second and unsurprisingly, this is the belief system that stops people living the life that they truly desire.

Here is an example in a business context:

Naomi has just qualified as a massage therapist and has her first paying client. She is nervous because she has never massaged a paying client before, even though Naomi has massaged hundreds of people throughout her training. She lacks confidence and is worried that the client will be able to tell and think that she is inexperienced (limiting beliefs).

The client, however, has no idea that they are Naomi's first paying client, they have just booked a massage and are coming to have their aches and pains soothed away. Naomi has been worrying so much in the run up to the appointment that when her client arrives, she is not actually ready. Naomi then mumbles an apology to her client about the delay and scuttles off to get her room ready. This event reaffirms her belief that she is inexperienced. When the appointment does finally start, Naomi's body language is closed and she seems to momentarily forget all her training. After ten minutes, the client appears irritated and asks Naomi how long she has been a massage therapist. At this

point, Naomi breaks down because the client's question is enough to confirm her self limiting beliefs.

An alternative example:

Lisa attended the same massage therapist training school as Naomi and is about to see her first paying client. Although Lisa is slightly nervous, she is also extremely excited about being able to put all of her hard work and training experience into practice with a paying client. Prior to the appointment, Lisa has allowed extra time to make sure her room is set-up and that everything is ready. When her client arrives, she is there to greet them and accompanies them to her room. Lisa then discusses the upcoming session with the client to ensure the client's expectations are met. During the appointment, Lisa continually checks with her client to ascertain if they are comfortable. At the end of the session, Lisa is confident that her client is satisfied which is reaffirmed by her client booking another appointment for the following week.

Both Lisa and Naomi had exactly the same training and experience; the only difference was, when placed in exactly the same situation, Lisa had belief in herself and her ability but Naomi did not.

There are three keys steps to overcoming these limiting beliefs:

1. Identify a belief that is holding you back.

2. Understand how it is affecting you and observe exactly how these beliefs are influencing your life;

    a. Think about the consequences of having this belief

    b. Do not be tempted to dwell in the past and try to unravel why you are how you are in this context. Trying to understand and make sense of your past could last you a lifetime and you could just get stuck.

    c. Be aware of how these thoughts affect you in the present. Understand if the thoughts have an empowering or disempowering effect.

3. Recondition your beliefs. Take action to address them and clear any disempowering thoughts or blocks from your mind.

Here is a simple exercise that will help you to address and change some of those old beliefs into new, more supportive ones:

- Make a list of the beliefs you have that may not be serving you well now.

- Ask yourself if these beliefs are ones you want to believe.

- Rewrite these beliefs as you would like them to be, changing each negative to a positive. For example, if one of your current limiting beliefs is: "It will be hard to attract new clients", it can be changed to "I can easily attract new clients", "I don't like selling and promoting", can be changed to "I love selling and promoting myself, so I am able to help more people."

- Write that new belief on a card and carry it around with you. Whenever the old beliefs surface, take out the card and read it to yourself. Read it often until you really believe that it is possible.

- You may have more than one belief that you wish to change. If this is the case, write each of them on the card. When you truly believe the new belief, you can cross it off your list.

If you do this whenever you discover a belief that does not help you, you will be removing some of the biggest obstacles on your journey to success.

Remember, almost all successful business owners have a set of beliefs that support them and their business objectives and there is no reason why this cannot be true for you.

The key reason why money is tight

Not charging enough for your time and/or giving away too much for free is common place in business.

The number one priority today for most business owners is to demonstrate their value to clients. As a result, many people are putting a huge amount of time and energy into exploring ways to heighten the value that they provide.

In today's value-focused world, everyone wants to get fair value. The issue comes down to the definition of value. Good value to one person could be considered overcharging by the next.

People often hold the belief that customers will not buy from them if they put their prices up. You probably hold this belief if you answer yes to any of the following statements:

- Your price list has not changed since you started your business.

- You compare yourself with the leaders in your niche market and conclude that you cannot compete with them; therefore, you have no right to charge what they do.

- You try to attract buyers by holding a sale too regularly, this screams desperation.

- You only sell cheap products and make it your Unique Selling Point, competing on price rather than quality.

Let us examine why people, particularly women, seem to find it so hard to ask for more money. I believe there are three key reasons. Firstly, we want to be liked. We fear that if we raise our rates, our clients, and potential clients, might not like it and they might not like us. Secondly, we fear that we might lose potential business or customers. Finally, many of us form long-lasting relationships with the people we sell to, and thinking about them feeling cross or upset over a rate change, or worse, walking away, is a hard pill to swallow.

All our beliefs are stored in the subconscious mind. Therefore, if you find that you are unable to make lots of money, or if you make money but are unable to hold on to it, it may be due to beliefs held in your subconscious mind. These could resemble "I do not deserve to be prosperous" or "Money is bad." In order to change our beliefs, we have to operate at the level of the subconscious mind.

The subconscious mind is your computer. It accepts an input, processes it and gives an output. It does not think by itself. It does not distinguish between good and bad. If we put rubbish in our computer, we get rubbish as the output.

Let us take a moment to look at your current associations with money. Read the statements below and circle every one you have heard or believe to be true:

- Money is the route of all evil.
- Rich people are not happy.
- It is more enlightening to be poor than rich.
- Rich people are greedy.
- As a woman, it is more difficult to get rich.
- I am too old to get rich.
- I am too young be rich.
- I am not educated enough to be rich.
- You cannot make money doing exactly what you love.
- Money is not really that important .
- Having a lot of money will make me less spiritual or pure.

- I wish I did not have to deal with money.
- Money causes problems.
- Money does not buy you love.

Now take a look over the statements you have circled and consider how these statements might be playing a part in your relationship with money. Are there any more examples you can think of?

It takes a strong sense of self to believe that we are worth a lot of money, and asking for more money pushes us out of our comfort zone. When we force ourselves to leave our comfort zone, we find that our comfort zone expands. Under-earners have a notoriously difficult time leaving their comfort zone, but they must venture out of it, if they wish to succeed in business.

So how do you know how high to raise your rates? It is not an exact science, but 'price resistance' is always a good starting point. Put simply if everyone can afford you and no one complains about your price, you are not charging enough. If everyone complains that you are charging too much, you are. Roughly ten percent of people will always complain about any price. After you lose the ten percent that always complain about cost, note how often you encounter price resistance. Remember that the point is not to offer a service or product that absolutely every person can afford. If that is the case, you need to increase what you charge. People value what they pay for, if you do not charge enough, they may feel that they are getting an inferior product or service.

It may also help you to create affirmations around money. For example, if you feel that you are worth more than you currently charge, you could develop an affirmation that you repeat to yourself. This must be in the present tense and should include an amount that you feel you are worth. Yes, you might feel silly saying this to yourself at first but by creating a positive statement, and repeating it, you will have a positive effect on your life and your business.

I was introduced to the idea of positive affirmations surrounding money at a T.Harv Eker event. At the time I didn't consider myself to have any issues with money, however as we went through the exercise I discovered that I had a number of negative beliefs that were undoubtedly holding me back. Having identified these beliefs I was able to create a set of personal affirmations which have definitely had a positive impact on my relationship with money and helped me in my business. Remember you affirmations must always be stated in the present tense.

 People value what they pay for, if you do not charge enough, they may feel that they are getting an inferior product or service."
- Phil M Jones

Why time is always short

 Your time is limited, so don't waste it living someone else's life. Don't be trapped by dogma – which is living with the results of other people's thinking. Don't let the noise of other's opinions drown out your own inner voice. And most importantly, have the courage to follow your heart and intuition. They somehow already know what you truly want to become. Everything else is secondary."
- Steve Jobs

With our hectic schedules and the never ending cycle of distractions in today's society, it is no surprise that so many of us struggle with time management.

However, although it cannot be denied that we lead very busy lives, we must also be aware that lack of time can often be used as an excuse for not getting things done. Telling ourselves we did not complete the task in question due to lack of time, makes us feel better.

When people feel overwhelmed with their work load it often leads to procrastination. The old saying: "I can't see the wood for the trees" is particularly relevant here. I am sure everyone can think about a time when there was so much to do that it was unclear where and how to begin the task and, as a result, nothing was achieved. Another common place where procrastination seems to rear its ugly head is when something extremely important needs to be completed yet somehow everything else is tackled but the task in hand.

I remember growing up, I was a typical teenage girl, my room was always a mess and my mum was constantly nagging me to tidy it up. I used to try every trick in the book to avoid tiding my room; however, when the time came to revise for my GCSE exams, suddenly I found that the most important thing was to tidy my room – procrastination took over.

Nowadays, with the latest technology at our fingertips and the advent of Facebook, Twitter and Instagram to keep us entertained, it is even harder to stay on task.

Common symptoms of poor time management

Lots of emails in your inbox – Your email inbox is out of control. You never manage to get it anywhere near close to zero. People are constantly chasing you for a response because they have not heard from you.

Clutter - Your office and/or home is a mess. You can barely see your desk because of all the papers, unpaid bills and credit card statements covering the surface. You feel there is no way that you are able to concentrate (or fulfill) the tasks at hand today. You can barely even see them for the mess.

Unfulfilled commitments - You are constantly running late or finding yourself cancelling or postponing appointments. You make promises you are unable to keep and find yourself always apologising.

Lack of the personal touch - People complain that they never hear from you. You are unable to make time for family and friends.

Stress - You constantly feel stressed, no matter how much work you complete. You always feel that you could be doing more and are never 'on top' of things.

If you found yourself relating to some or even all the statements above, you must not feel ashamed. In western culture, these feelings are almost inevitable. However, you can take control of your schedule, and you need to do so if you are to be an effective business person.

Here are some tips on where you can make the small changes that will make a huge difference:

Lots of emails in your inbox

The first step towards having an organised inbox is to set up a simple and effective email system. Separate your emails into two main categories - Reference and Action:

- **Reference** – These are information emails that do not require any action but contain information that is important.

- **Action** – These are emails that require an action. Action emails should be stored either on your to-do list or in your calendar.

Most people receive a considerable amount (sometimes as much as a third) of reference information through email. It is, therefore, essential to have a system that makes it easy to transfer messages from your inbox into your email reference system - a series of email file folders where you store reference information to ensure you have easy access to it later.

Schedule a specific time during the day to process and organise your emails. It is nearly impossible to complete anything when there are constant interruptions from the phone, people stopping by your office, and instant messaging; it is, therefore, critical that you set aside uninterrupted time to process and organise your emails.

Many email messages require you to make a decision; decisions require focus; focus requires uninterrupted attention. Establish a regular time each day to process your email so that you can empty your inbox.

Book yourself a recurring appointment for an hour a day to process email, and mark that time as 'busy' in your calendar. During that hour, you must not answer the phone or take interruptions and you must work solely on processing your inbox. When you sit down to process your email, the first step is to sort it by the order in which it will be processed. Resist the temptation to jump around in your inbox in no particular order. Begin processing the message at the top of your inbox, and only move to the second one after you have handled the first. This can be hard at first, when you might have thousands of messages in your inbox, but as you reduce the number of emails over a few sessions, and regularly get your inbox down to zero, it will become easier and even a pleasure.

Finally, use the 'Four Ds for Decision-Making' model to process your emails

- Delete it
- Do it
- Delegate it
- Defer it

Using the 'Four Ds' model on a daily basis makes it easier to handle a large quantity of email. To help reduce the number of unnecessary emails arriving in your inbox, consider unsubscribing from email newsletters that you never subscribed to in the first place and ask colleagues and friends to remove your name from their email blasts which bombard you with unnecessary information.

Clutter

Clutter comes at a price. It may not be immediately obvious to us but the more that we accumulate the more that our clutter begins to demand of us. Be aware that how you live on the outside, you are likely to live on the inside too. Therefore, if your environment is cluttered, it is likely that your mind is also cluttered. This is probably why so many people suffer from procrastination and indecisiveness, and feel totally overwhelmed on a regular basis. Getting rid of the clutter clears your mind and allows your genius to shine through.

Here are a few simple tips for you to eliminate clutter and transform your day to day living:

- **Sort through your papers and mail everyday**
  * Open your post over a bin and either file it, shred it or put in the recycling bin.
  * If it is a bill, resist the temptation to ignore it and leave it lying around unopened – open it and deal with it.
  * If you spend just five minutes a day going through your post, this will be one less chore to be done at the weekend and leaves more time for fun and relaxation.

- **Set up a system to handle your incoming papers**. Make a decision as to what needs to be done with them – discard, delegate, take immediate action, file for follow-up, or archive for future reference.

- **Gather any existing papers together and again make a decision as to what needs to be done with them** – discard, delegate, take immediate action, file for follow up, or archive for future reference.

- **Ensure you prioritise and keep the most important paper to action at the top**; the same applies to your reference pile. If you do this, when you begin to deal with the paperwork, you will be looking at the highest priority first.

- **Clearly label** containers, shelves, bookcases, and any other items that will help others to know where items belong.

- **Look around your office**. If there is any broken equipment, chairs, files, or any outdated technology that is not used, then make time to donate or dispose of these items.

- **Do not use the "just in case, you never know, or someday maybe it will be useful" reasons** to continue to hold onto things. Whether it is equipment, papers or ideas — clear out, clean out and make room for the new.

- **Just do it!** How long are you going to spend planning and thinking about that new project? Make a list of what you need to do to move on that new idea and do not waste any more time. You cannot finish something that you have never started.

Unfulfilled commitments

Our old friend, or should I say our worst enemy, procrastination is often the culprit here. Through lack of proper planning and a feeling of being overwhelmed, it is very easy to find that you have bitten off more than you can chew. We all know that being late, missing or canceling appointments and breaking promises only makes us feel bad. It is, therefore, important to put in place systems that avoid this happening.

The secret here is simple and it is all down to planning. Here is the four step process that will ensure success:

1. Brainstorm your weekly tasks

My personal preference for doing weekly planning is on a Sunday. The first thing you do is brainstorm all the tasks that you want to do the following week and put them into a list, then divide the list into two categories – Professional and Personal.

2. Set priorities

The next step is to decide what is most important this week. This means to set priorities within your tasks. I use the following system and have found it to be very effective:

- **Priority A:** Must get done.
- **Priority B:** Should get done.
- **Priority C:** Nice to have done.

All Priority A tasks must get done within the week, there are no exceptions. This means that you start with Priority A tasks and finish them, before you begin Priority B, or even contemplate Priority C tasks.

3. Put your tasks into your calendar

Put the tasks into your calendar and lock-in time to complete them. Your calendar should be your number one organisational tool. I use my Microsoft Outlook Calendar, which is synced with my mobile phone; however, you can use any calendar such as Firefox, iCal (on Apple) or Google Calendar. I also still like to keep a paper diary with me.

Make sure you leave time open in your calendar. I keep 20% free every day, so that I can react to what is happening on a daily basis.

4. Execute

Start executing your Priority A tasks on Monday and work along your calendar schedule. Try to focus on one task at a time. If you get interrupted and are not able to prevent it (remember you don't have to take every phone-call), focus on that new task and then return to your current task as soon as possible.

If you have to reschedule then do so, but make sure that you keep your Priority A tasks to the front. The most important thing is to get all As done within the week. Then advance to the Bs and finally to the Cs.

The result of this weekly planning and executing around your personal life priorities is simply that you will make significant progress in your chosen direction. You will make good progress in the week and huge progress over the months and years that follow.

Extra tip: Before you go to bed write down everything you need to do the following day, and then circle the top three items that you MUST achieve the following day to feel satisfied. By doing this, you know exactly what you need to concentrate on as a priority in the morning, which helps stop the feeling of being overwhelmed. This will also help you to sleep better, as you have offloaded thoughts from your head onto paper.

Lack of the personal touch

Losing touch with those who are closest to you is a clear sign that you are spending too much time at work or are too engrossed in an activity. There is nothing wrong with being passionate and wanting to work hard, however, it is important that you take time out to relax and enjoy life. By doing this you will find you are more productive at work and much, much happier.

However, a word of warning, taking time out does not mean that you should arrange to meet up with your friends and family, and spend the whole time answering your emails and making calls on your mobile.

The best advice is to make sure that you make time for your family and friends. Schedule it into your day, week, month and stick to it. Plan when you are going to call your parents each week and make it a habit. Remember, life is not a dress rehearsal.

Another thing that I find helpful, and I know the thought of this might bring you out in a cold sweat, is to leave your mobile at home, or at the very least switch it off when you are concentrating on a task. It is surprisingly liberating to be unavailable, even if it is just for an hour.

Stress

Every single one of us will feel stressed from time to time when we feel under too much mental or emotional pressure.

People react differently to stress, so something that feels stressful to one person may be motivating to another. Stress can affect how you think, feel, behave and how your body works. The most common signs of stress include loss of appetite, sleep disturbance and difficulty concentrating. There is little you can do to prevent stress but there are many things you can do to manage stress more effectively. Here are a few of my favourite stress busters:

• **Change your state**

By altering your body's physiology, you can achieve an immediate change of your emotional state. The mind will follow whatever state your physical body is in, and not vice-versa. If the state you are in is not serving you in a positive manner, change it. It takes practise but when you master it, it will transform your life.

• **Take control**

Feeling a loss of control is a major cause of stress. If you remain passive and think that you cannot do anything about your problem, your stress will get worse. Remember there is a solution to any problem. The act of taking control is in itself empowering, and it is crucial to find a solution that satisfies you and not someone else.

• Be active

When we exercise our bodies it releases the chemicals endorphins, adrenaline, serotonin, and dopamine. These chemicals work together to make us feel good. Physical activity can help us to get into the right state of mind to be able to identify the cause of our stress and find a solution. Exercise will not make stress disappear but it will reduce some of the emotional intensity, allowing a clearing of the mind and enabling a calmer approach to problems.

• Connect with people

When people are stressed they have a tendency to become ostrich-like and bury their heads in the sand but this only makes things worse. A good support network of friends, family and colleagues can ease your work troubles and help you to see things in a different way. There really is no better stress relief than having a laugh with your friends.

• Have some "me time"

We all need to take time out to do something that we enjoy. Make a point of setting aside a couple of nights a week for some quality 'me time' away from work. Diarise those two dates and stick to them – they will give you a break from work and some helpful perspective.

• **Challenge yourself**

Setting yourself goals and challenges, whether at work or outside it, helps to build confidence and will help you deal with stress.

• **Be positive**

Look for the positives in life, and things for which you are grateful. At the end of each day, write down at least three things that went well. This will require a shift in perspective for those who are more naturally pessimistic; however, by making a conscious effort, you can train yourself to be more positive about life. Problems are often a question of perspective. If you change your perspective, you change your viewpoint. Remember nothing has meaning except from the meaning we imbue it with.

• **Accept the things you cannot change**

Learn to let go of situations which are out of your control. Changing a difficult situation is not always possible. If this proves to be the case, you must recognise this, accept it and move on. Concentrate on the things which you can control and do not dwell on those things which are out of your control.

The importance of planning

Every business decision you make today affects your business today, tomorrow, and in the future. You need to develop good strategic skills. A good strategist looks at all facets of their business today, in the context of what they are trying to build their business towards. A good strategist reacts to problems positively and welcomes change, transforming it into an opportunity. A good strategist can also react quickly and well to the unexpected.

The most common questions I am asked when people are starting a new business are: "Do I really need a business plan?" "Is writing a business plan really the best use of my time?" My answer to these questions is always, "Yes". Even if you don't require funding, you still need to have a business plan.

If you are raising capital or taking on a lot of risk; for example, leaving employment, investing savings or supporting a family, you will need to plan your business in great detail. If you are doing none of these things, less detail is acceptable.

Business plans are one of the most effective tools for the business owner who is starting, growing and even managing a business for three reasons:

- They give business owners a current assessment of the business and a roadmap for the future.

- They help a business grow, both organically and through outside funding.

- They help secure and maintain finance, ranging from an overdraft facility or bank loan, to venture capital funding.

If you are planning to approach a financial institution for a loan, apply for a small business grant, pitch your business idea to investors, or enlist the support of a business partner; a business plan is required.

There are some sections in a traditional business plan that you cannot complete if you have not decided on, or are not fully committed to, a certain aspect of the business. A business plan forces you to write down specific information in black and white and this will help you to eliminate any of these grey areas. This forces you to make tough decisions and is often one of the hardest and most useful aspects of writing a business plan.

Small business owners might find writing a business plan the first real struggle that they have encountered, as they are not ready to consider that their business idea might be a bit flawed or is not yet fully developed. Whilst this is an unwelcome and terrifying thought for an impassioned entrepreneur, identifying gaps early on in the process gives business owners the chance to support their research, test their ideas and take steps to make the business stronger and more viable. This may initially be a step back but any and all further work can reinforce the entrepreneur's chance of success before he or she invests time and money in a business that is likely to fail.

The last thing you want to do is work on your start-up for a year, only to realise that you were doomed to fail from the start. Many founders learn the hard way that they did not set aside enough capital to reach their goals, took on partners with the wrong skills and resources, or did not have a viable way to make money. Developing and sharing a business plan can help ensure that you are sprinting down the right path not languishing in a ditch.

At times during your start-up experience, you will be manic, becoming so passionate about your ideas that you lose sight of reality. At other times, you will be overwhelmed by doubt, fear or exhaustion. When your emotions get the better of you, having a business plan enables you to step back, and take an objective look at what you are doing and why. Discovering new ideas, different approaches and fresh perspectives are some of the best things that can happen during the business planning process. An effective business plan is a flexible, growing and dynamic tool that can help you think creatively and arrive at new solutions for some of your toughest business challenges.

The exercise below provides a quick and painless start to the business planning process. Asking yourself a series of questions about your business, your goals and your future plans will result in a streamlined and brief business plan that you can use immediately, or as a starting point for a more traditional business plan.

Business Planning Exercise
Time Required: Approximately 2-3 Hours

- **Outline the vision you have for your business by answering these questions:**
    - * What are you creating?
    - * What will your business look like in:
        - ◊ One year,

◇ Three years,

◇ Five years?

- **What is your mission?**
  - * Why are you starting this business
  - * What is its purpose?

- **List your overall objectives by outlining your most important business goals, and answering this question:**
  - * Are your business goals SMART (Specific, Measurable, Attainable, Realistic, Timely)?

- **Write down your business strategies by answering these questions:**
  - * How are you going to build your business?
  - * What will you sell?
  - * What is your Unique Selling Point (what makes your business different from the competition)?

- **What is the total start-up capital you will need to launch your business?**

- **What do you estimate your business' ongoing monthly expenses will be:**
  - * Immediately after launch,
  - * in three months,
  - * in six months,
  - * in one year?

- **What do you anticipate your business' ongoing monthly income will be:**
    * Immediately after launch,
    * in three months,
    * in six months,
    * in one year?

- **Create an action plan by answering:**
    * What are the specific action items and tasks you need to complete now?
    * What are your future milestones?
    * What will need to be accomplished by those milestones in order to meet your objectives?

If, after completing the above exercise, you wish to develop a more traditional business plan, below is the outline of the sections in the order that they typically appear:

• Executive Summary

The executive summary is the first section of your small business plan. It is usually written last and it provides an overview of all the other sections in the business plan.

• Company Description

The company description outlines vital details about your

company, such as where you are located, how large the company is, what you do and what you hope to accomplish.

• Products and/or Services

In this section, you should clearly describe the products and/or services that you will be selling. Emphasise the value and quality that you are providing your customers or clients with.

• Market Analysis

In this section, you should provide a detailed overview of the industry in which you intend to sell your product or service, including statistics to support your claims.

• Market Strategy

This section of the business plan builds on the market analysis section. It should outline where your business fits into the market and how you will price, promote and sell your product or service.

• Management Summary

The management summary section of your business plan describes how your business is structured, introduces who is involved, outlines external resources and explains how the business will be managed.

• Financial Analysis

The financial analysis section of your business plan should contain the details for financing your business now, what will be needed for future growth and an estimation of operating costs.

• Appendix and Supporting Information

The appendix to your business plan includes information that supports your statements, assumptions and the reasoning you have used in the other sections of your business plan. This may include graphs, charts, statistics, photos, marketing materials, research and other relevant data.

Why business is a team game

Believing that you can do everything by yourself is probably one of the greatest, if not the greatest mistake you can make in business. You can do everything, however, it is very likely that if you are doing this, you are doing everything poorly, spreading yourself too thinly and embodying the phrase '"Jack of all trades, master of none".

If you imagine an evening at the theatre you cannot just think of the bricks and mortar, but of the number of resources required to make the theatre experience. Those involved at the 'front of house' and those at the 'back of house'. At the front of house, there are ticket sales assistants, ushers, performers, directors and all the beautiful sets and scenes; all those things that belong to the experiential part of your visit. At the back of house, there are those behind the scenes 'resources': make-up artists, dressers, props, runners and all the administration and operations that combine to create that special experience of a night at the theatre.

Business is no different; there are so many 'behind-the-scenes' elements to running a business that if you truly want to succeed you must accept that you are not able to do them all by yourself, how ever much you would like to control every aspect of your business. No matter what level of business you are in, you need the right resources, the right team and the right systems to create the leverage to help your business to grow to the next level.

The reason that I am so aware of this mistake is that for many years I have been guilty of making it myself. When I first started my own business, I wanted to do everything. I thought that this would help me to both keep the costs down and to remain in complete control.

The reality was that I wasted months creating a website which looked mediocre and unprofessional, weeks creating ordinary marketing materials, and precious days focusing on all the minutiae involved in business instead of actually focusing on what really mattered - building the business. If I had actually calculated what my time had cost me to do all these things, I could have paid a professional to do them ten times over and ten times better. In reality, I was no longer controlling my business, it was controlling me.

So here is a newsflash, just like any other person you will have one or two natural talents and if you do not concentrate solely on these talents, your business will suffer.

Firstly, you must identify your natural talents and focus on them so that you are able to achieve their fullest potential. This in itself might be easier said than done. You might even struggle to

identify your true natural talents, as we are often very hard on ourselves and find it easier to criticise than to think about what we are good at. If you do experience this, I suggest you take a piece of paper and begin by writing down anything that comes into your head that you think you are good at in a business context, no matter how insignificant it seems. Once you have your list, circle the two that you think you are the best at. You can ask others for their opinions however, you must remember that it should be you who identifies your top two talents; otherwise you will have somebody else's perception of your talents rather than your own.

 Secondly, surround yourself with people who are strong where your talents are at their weakest (your list will help with this) and build a solid network of trusted, talented people. Great companies are built on the foundation of exploiting a few strengths, not on trying to be masters of everything.

In order for your business to grow (and with it your income), you need time to focus on what will actually attract more clients and income. To achieve more time in your solo business you need leverage. Leverage involves employing the necessary resources (people, systems, automation and delegation) to free up your time so that you are able to focus on money-generating activities (client work, marketing, business development). Once you master leverage in your business, you will no longer just own a business but be a business owner.

How to leverage your business:

1. Make a list of all the tasks that you undertake during the day.

2. Add a cost amount to each item that you could pay someone else to do for you; for example errands, post and phone calls. It is actually less expensive than you think.

3. Group similar tasks together by cost-amount and then by category (website, administrative, personal)

4. Identify the tasks within your business that only YOU can do. Next consider which tasks you could hire someone else to do. The internet has made it extremely easy to find talented freelancers and hire them at the click of a button. A few websites you could use include: PeoplePerHour.com and fiverr.com. You can

browse profiles and decide who you want to hire based on their experience and ratings from other users. If you are looking for more permanent support for your business gumtree.com and craigslist.com are great websites to post a local job advert.

5. Delegate the lowest cost tasks first and focus this newly available time on further business development, marketing to your ideal clients and making room for more clients.

How to be seen by more of the right kind of people

Like it or not, if your business does not have a web presence, then your business is invisible to a large portion of your potential new clients.

Although, you are probably aware of some businesses which are doing incredibly well without a website, I often wonder how much better they could be doing if they took the time to invest in an internet presence. By website, I mean a legitimate, well-thought-out site that is designed to inform, engage and convert the audience.

There was a time when only large, established businesses had websites; most small business promotion was still done through advertisements and brochures. However, consumers now go online first to seek information on local businesses. Almost every successful company has at least a basic website, where customers can find out about products and services, and obtain contact information.

Your relationship with your clients is one of trust, much like that of a Personal Trainer or Massage Therapist. To feel comfortable enough to do business with you, potential clients want to know how you operate and which services you offer. Viewing a website is a non-confrontational way for potential clients to get a feel for who you are and what you can do for them. They can read about other happy clients and the difference you have made to their lives; it is an important way for your clients to get to know you and feel comfortable with their choice.

When choosing, for example, a Personal Trainer we know that potential clients will often look at multiple trainers, in order to choose the one who is most closely aligned with their needs. The easiest way for a person to do this is by comparing websites.

Therefore, if you do not have a website, you are immediately at a disadvantage. A website with basic brochure-style information on it is useful but if you have a robust site with articles, advice, client testimonials and other interesting tools, you are more likely to catch the eye of a new client.

While many clients may already know your name before they begin their search, some will search for local organisations on the internet and, if your business name does not appear in search results, you will miss out on customers and income. An experienced web designer understands how to make your site prominent in online search results and it is worth the investment to hire one. Ranking high in search results also gives your firm an established appearance.

You also need to consider whether or not your website is mobile optimised. If it is not then you are again invisible to a large number of clients who will only ever search the web via their mobile phones. These potential clients will just go to your competitors, who have already made the move to a mobile optimised site.

Maintaining a website is an easy way to gather clients email addresses and other contact and personal information. There are several electronic newsletter applications that you can link to your site; clients enter their information and are automatically signed up for future communications from you. This way, you can reach your clients whenever you want to, in order to let them know about new services or other company news. The automated system saves you the substantial amount of time it would take you to accumulate, sort and copy the information by hand.

All things Social

Many business owners, particularly small business owners, still feel that social media is not important to their business. This mindset is costing them thousands of pounds in potential business sales. The rise in the number of people who use social media means that businesses are now put in a situation where they must have a social media presence, in order to interact closely with their customers.

Social media is extremely important and when you get your business presence right, it can help to grow your business exponentially. However, to establish your business as social, you need to participate in social media on a regular basis. One way to achieve this is by embracing social media technologies across all levels of your business. Only by letting social media infiltrate through all the established structures, will your business be able to convince your customers it has not been left behind.

Social media has become an extremely competitive space because it is being embraced by so many businesses. The good news is that there is room for everybody. Customers currently base how 'social' you are, and how good your business is, by comparing your Facebook fans, Twitter followers and subscribers.

The only way to succeed in social media is to become more creative and experimental and this needs to filter through all areas of your business.

Once you have established yourself as a social business, you will see an increase in efficiency, brainstorming, product development and so much more. How do you find out what your customers want from your next product? You ask them. Social media allows businesses to take the advantage of platforms like Twitter and Facebook and obtain some free and relevant feedback within minutes.

Your customers use social media everyday and so should your business. Your customers live much of their lives through social media; they interact with it by sharing ideas and findings. Live your business the way they live their lives on social media and do not be tempted to use social media as merely a blunt advertising tool by just badly presenting your products. Social media is a way of being reactive, open and collaborative. Being in control of every tiny detail is not always best way to encourage custom; embracing social platforms and encouraging debate and feedback is the best way to connect with your customers.

You might find social media a little daunting but it is here to stay and is set to become more widespread. Therefore, the faster you embrace this global network, the better for you and your growing business.

The Biggest Social Media Sites:

When thinking about social media for business, one cannot ignore Facebook; it is a social media giant that in 2012 reached more than 900 million users. Facebook handles around 1 billion search queries a day and is one of the key social media sites used by businesses to connect with other clients and other businesses.

Although Facebook does not allow businesses to have a profile, it is possible to create a page where you can let clients know about your latest discounts, any events that you are attending and more information about your business. Clients can also follow the activity of the business and invite friends to share in the business' Facebook feed.

Another social media site which has gained a lot of interest for business purposes is Twitter. Although Twitter is sometimes considered by many people to be a 'celebrity following' tool, many businesses have harnessed Twitter's ability to share information in a quick and seamless fashion. Twitter has fewer boundaries than Facebook, there are limited privacy settings and therefore people can follow you on Twitter without needing your acceptance. This means that you can quickly gain more followers as the weeks go on. You can then use this social media site to Tweet about your latest events.

You should spend time seeking out the influential people and accounts in your business sector and reach out to them. This will help you to be on the radar of their customers, who could also be your next customers. Be sure to re-Tweet things that will interest your followers and things from the influencers; this will assist with your profile as an information sharer.

The more you use the social networking sites, the better for your business. Your website must also correspond to your social media sites. This will encourage your website visitors to follow your brand, meaning you have access to them whenever you like. They will not need to visit your website every time to be presented with information about your business and industry. People generally log into their social networks many times each day but may only visit your website once. This means that through social media you could gain a lifetime customer who you would not otherwise have reached if you had not organised a social presence.

By linking your sites, you increase your search engine optimisation. This means that your sites can start to appear in search engine results like Google when more and different keywords are used in the search criteria. This will increase your website traffic, which will result in more sales and/or leads.

Social media sites can make your business and brand global – even if you are just a small start-up firm, so you really have every reason to add social media to your business model.

The secret reason why customers are not coming back

 The single, most powerful way that you can influence what your customers say about you is through how you treat them."

In today's environment, everyone is an author. Any of your customers could write about your product or service on his or her blog, Facebook wall, Twitter account or anywhere else. It is, therefore, imperative to put the customer first at all times.

If we look at an example of a successful hairdresser, it will help to illustrate how a successful business brilliantly communicates with its customers:

You have booked an appointment at a salon and the day before your appointment you receive a phone call from the salon checking everything is still ok for your appointment the following day (thus making sure that you are committed to attending the appointment).

When you arrive at the salon, you are greeted by name and asked if your coat can be taken and if you would like a drink. If for any reason your hairdresser is running behind, then they personally ensure that you have been notified. At the start of your appointment, the hairdresser will confirm with you exactly what you would like them to do with your hair that day. You are reassured by their confidence. If you are not sure what you would like the hairdresser to do with your hair, or you are considering a new style, your hairdresser will discuss this with you and give you their honest advice until you feel completely comfortable with your choice. During your appointment, your hairdresser will ask you all about you and your life. If you are a returning customer, they will always pick up the conversation where it was left on your last visit.

When it comes to the actual haircut, your hairdresser will again obtain confirmation from you that you are happy with the cut. When the appointment has finished they use a mirror to show you your new style from all angles and get a final confirmation from you that you are happy. They then compliment you on how fantastic your hair looks and ask you if you would like your next appointment in 6 or 8 weeks. The successful hairdresser makes sure that you do not leave the salon that day without having your next appointment booked in.

Between appointments you will receive offers from the salon encouraging you to refer a friend and receive a discount off your next appointment. This is a win-win situation for both parties –

you receive a discount and the salon achieves a new customer via a satisfied customer's referral. I cannot think of a better example of a business controlling their customers.

Referrals are so effective because they come from a credible third-party who has first hand experience of the benefits of doing business with you. They become even more powerful when the referral is from a friend because you know that a friend has no ulterior motive. As a customer, you are much more likely to believe a friend's recommendation, compared with the recommendation of a salesperson whose raison d'être is to take money from you and receive a commission for themselves.

Referrals are also valuable because most of the time they are completely free. It is comparable to receiving the benefit of the most compelling sales advertisement on earth for absolutely nothing.

Finally, customers who give referrals tend to become more loyal. Once someone makes a public statement about you, psychologically they will become more loyal to you and your business because they have made an emotional and physical investment in the business.

Although customer service is critical to the success of your referral programme, it does not necessarily mean that you will get a lot of referrals. Many small business owners assume that referrals will just happen provided that they give good customer service, however this is not true. If you are not proactive in creating referrals, the chances of you receiving the abundance of referrals you desire and deserve are slim. Your best customers are ready and willing to give you referrals, you just need to show them how.

There are two main sources for referrals; your current customers (people who have done business with you) and other influential people. You should ensure that you have an active referral system for both types of people. Your referral system needs to be a methodically planned process that you have put in place to capture qualified prospects through your association with other people. You should be able to turn this system on and off like a light switch, with a clear understanding of what the results will be.

To get more referrals you must ask for them. This sounds simple but in reality although business owners know that they need to ask for referrals to get more referrals, the fear of asking often inhibits them from moving forward. If you hold a self-limiting belief that you are asking that person to go out on a limb for you by asking them to give you a referral, you will always be battling with fear. However, if you truly believe that it will be helping them by asking them to give you referrals; your fear will quickly fade. Your customers want to give you referrals. It makes them feel good about themselves to share positive experiences with other people; you must not miss out on any opportunity to get these precious referrals.

So how exactly do you ask for a referral? The chances are if you have ever been asked for a referral it has played out like this: "Hey, you wouldn't happen to you know anyone who could benefit from my services would you?" They pause to think for a few seconds and say, "I can't think of anyone off the top of my head, but I will keep it in mind." Unfortunately, if you are asking for your referrals in this way you might as well not ask the question at all. It is highly unlikely that you will get a positive response to this question because the question was not asked correctly. People need a frame of reference to help them narrow down the playing field of potential referral candidates. By simply narrowing the frame of reference you can allow them to visualise any potential referrals in their mind. This may be limiting the number of potential people that they might know, but it is far more effective than opening up the flood gates of people they might know, but cannot remember.

Here is a list of ideas that you can use to create your own referral system:

- Create a referral program with service providers to exchange referrals. Be sure that you only include providers in this network that you would be comfortable recommending to your best client or best friend.

- Recognise and thank your referral sources. This could be with a simple phone call, email, or, even better, a handwritten note. The important thing is to express your appreciation. You will also encourage additional referrals this way.

- If you have clients who do not refer you, create another way for them to recommend your services instead; for example, via a case study or a testimonial.

- Include a 'referrals appreciated' paragraph in your print or email newsletter. Be sure to describe what an ideal referral looks like to you.

- In your email newsletter, include a request: "If this article helped you, please share it with your network e.g., Facebook, Twitter and LinkedIn." Add icons and links that make it easy to share content.

- Make sure that your current clients know about all the services you offer, so that they are able to make referrals within their company and to others outside. Too often providers assume their clients know more about them than they do.

- Add a link to a form on your website for referral submissions.

- Proactively refer people to other businesses that have a clientele similar to yours. Let those businesses know that you have referred them and that you would appreciate the same in return.

- Be outstanding! Remind clients why your service is special. Give them something (good) to talk about.

- Inspire confidence. It is risky referring someone - what if it is not successful? You can inspire confidence in your referral sources by letting them know that a percentage of your business comes from repeat customers.

- Offer an affiliate program.

- Inspire confidence by offering a guarantee.

- Provide valuable content which your referral sources can share with their network. Make it relevant and something special for them to share.

- Update your LinkedIn profile. Include the link to your profile in your email newsletter or website to make it easy for it to be shared by referral sources. Include it in your email signature with the note, "Please feel free to forward my profile to others who you feel would benefit from my services."

- Create a list of prospects you want to work with. Check out their LinkedIn profiles to see whether you are connected in any way. If so, reach out to them via your network, whether it is an individual, a company, or a group.

- Create a referral program for current clients, where they receive some type of reward or recognition for the new business they refer. This might be in the form of a discount voucher or buy 2-get-1-half price.

- Encourage conversation from Twitter, Facebook and other social networks, reach out to your networks online and request referrals. On Twitter, you can ask your followers to re-Tweet to their networks.

- Be helpful in forums. There are many stories of helpful people getting business just from the goodwill they create from helping on Twitter, LinkedIn and private online communities.

- Treat your customers as partners. Let them know you view them as a strategic partner, and tell them you hope that they will do the same for you. Create formal channels to share referrals.

- Give a referral. It is one of the best ways to get one in return.

Let these suggestions jump-start your own idea generation. Create a focused referral process that works for your ideal clients and your networks. By putting a referral system into place now, you are more likely to receive quality referrals throughout the year.

The fortune is in the follow-up

You may have heard the saying "the fortune is in the follow-up" and this is absolutely true. Business owners are often very good at reaching out to new customers. The problem arises when they fail to follow-up the sale or expression of interest because they do not want to seem pushy or come across as desperate for custom. However, while one business owner is worrying about annoying a prospective customer or telling themselves that the customer will return when they are ready, another business owner has already followed up and sealed the deal.

When someone expresses interest in your business, but they are not quite ready to sign on the dotted line, they can often be persuaded with a polite follow-up. It might be worth bearing in mind that studies have suggested that it takes an average of eight contacts with a prospect to convert a lead into a sale. Most people stop at two. With this in mind, it is essential that you manage your follow-up by tracking your contacts. There are many systems out there, the key is to choose one that works for you and use it.

Some suggested steps to implement for an effective follow-up strategy

Many people are great at follow-up in the first few months of initial contact or actually making the sale; however, follow-up thereafter often seems to drop off. Maintaining consistent follow-up or touch points through phone conversations, live appointments, email, newsletters and greeting cards should be the goal.

Train your customers to expect to hear from you by being consistent. Your clients will begin to expect to hear from you and will make time for you.

Make each contact lead to the next contact by letting your customer know when they will hear from you again. In any appointment or meeting with a customer, you try to schedule your next appointment/meeting before you leave. If you need to follow-up your meeting with additional information, you should ensure that the customer knows when they can expect to hear from you.

Assume that you, as the business owner, have the responsibility to make contact. It is your responsibility to maintain the relationship, not theirs, and remember that customers who do not feel appreciated will naturally start looking elsewhere. If you keep consistent contact with your customers and take responsibility for the relationship, this will help you to maintain your customers for life.

Create a plan and stick to it. If you are consistently following-up with your customers, your customers will naturally start contacting you. The key is to not break your consistency and to maintain that trusted relationship.

Once you have your plan to implement a system for leveraging your time, try to put each element of this into an automatic system. Automatically your newsletter should be posted every month; automatically your calendar should pop-up with a reminder to call a particular customer. By having a system in place, you guarantee consistency in your actions.

Why the phone is not ringing

If you want to have a successful and profitable business, then you need leads and lots of them. Nothing happens without a lead. No sales, no revenue, no profit, nothing. You cannot simply launch a website and wait for the phone to ring; you need to ensure that you have an effective lead generation system in place.

How do you generate your leads?

Put simply, lead generation is a marketing term used to describe the practice of seeking enquiries, from potential customers, into the products and/or services of a business. The leads are usually generated from a number of sources or activities, such as the internet, telephone calls, referrals, list purchase or advertisements. The quality of the lead is usually determined by the tendency of the enquirer to take action towards a purchase.

Lead Generation is not a new form of gaining new business, but it does now have a new approach. Traditionally, lead generation occurred at places like trade shows where visitors to a company's stand would complete a card with their contact information on and in turn they would receive a call back from that company's sales team. Since the rise of the internet, many businesses use this technology as another lead generation option.

Why use lead generation?

Lead generation is a win-win situation for both buyer and seller. A potential buyer is able to request information from several businesses that offer the products and/or service they desire, and the seller is given the opportunity to pitch their products and/or service to someone who has given them permission to do so. Conversion rates on "pre-qualified" leads often have a higher conversion success rate compared with cold leads.

Lead generation is the first step of the sales process and for this reason both quality and quantity need to be considered. As we know, quality leads are leads that a business owner has a good chance of closing. Every lead list will have a number of "junk leads" (people who are not qualified to buy the product for some reason) but the smaller the percentage of bad leads, the less time wasted while processing the list. Quantity is also important because even if you have a list of 100% good leads, you won't be able to close every one of them.

Lead generation techniques are usually a trade-off between quality and quantity. For example, a form on your website that visitors can complete to request a call back will generate high-quality leads from those people who are very likely to buy; however, this form of lead generation is unlikely to generate a large quantity of leads. On the other hand, a lead list that is based

on a newsletter subscription list from another company might generate a large quantity of leads, but these leads will not be nearly as interested or qualified. This trade-off is another reason why companies are wise to use many lead generation methods. In fact, most marketing experts recommend that companies use at least ten different lead generation methods to ensure that their communication lines remain full.

It is imperative that you understand the cost of your lead generation, as almost all forms of lead generation will produce leads but those leads will come at different costs. The trick is to quickly determine which channel/s produces the best leads for the least cost. You should approach lead generation in the same way that you would any other advertising campaign, set aside a reasonable budget to test it and see if it works for your business. The key to being successful in lead generation is to refresh your sales and marketing skills so that the leads you receive convert at a high sales rate. Do not try to approach this method of marketing without the ability to follow through and close the sale.

Traditional lead generation methods:

Some of the oldest ways to market any kind of product or service is through advertising in the newspapers, radio and television, local directories or by distributing your business cards. Promotional products are a traditional way of highlighting your company or your product to a wider variety of people, and there are an abundance of trade shows, seminars and workshops you can attend either as a delegate or an exhibitor to attract potential leads. Other offline marketing methods include direct mail, phone campaigns, or going door-to-door.

Generating leads using these traditional means can be time consuming and expensive, so it is important that you get it right. Test methods (small numbers at a time and then scale up) that are most appropriate for your business to determine which give the higher closing ratios for your business.

Direct mail is one of the most successful traditional lead generation methods however it is certainly not as simple as typing a letter, adding an address and stamp, and popping it in the mail.

There are some key golden rules to making your direct mailings work effectively. That doesn't mean that you have to spend more money in order to succeed, far from it. In fact, you could find yourself spending less or at least spending more strategically than you may be doing at present. Here's how:

Mail to Mr. Right

There is a simple but very clear distinction between junk mail and direct mail. Junk mail is mail isn't wanted, and direct mail is something that goes to the right person and is wanted. One major key to the success of your direct mailing is to find the right people to mail to. If you have gathered leads from a recent event or workshop this is a great place to start. However don't rely on anyone passing your mailer on, as it just won't happen! Make a telephone call to check that your information is up to date

Boost Your Letter

Once you've found out whom to send your letter to, your next step is to make sure that your letter works to its maximum effect. Write it as a one-on-one dialogue. Beware of using industry lingo that your prospect may not understand. Keep your paragraphs short and sweet - no more than seven lines. Break up your letter into clearly defined subheads and keep it to two pages in length.

Make All Your Copy Benefit-Oriented

List the benefits so they are easy to understand. Remember that a benefit is a lot different than a feature. Features do not have the clout that benefits do. For example, stating that "I offer bespoke one to one personal training & nutritional advice in the comfort of your own home" is merely a feature. Write it in the context of a benefit: "my clients lose weight and keep it off, why? Because I teach you to develop a positive relationship with food and exercise in the comfort of your own home, which will make you feel better than you ever have before - or your money back" and you'll start making the impact that you want.

Repeat your offer at least three times throughout your letter: In your headline, within the first two paragraphs, and again in your closing paragraph. You can also include it in a "p.s." Last, but not least, tell your prospects what the next step is and tell them to do it today. Also include details of where to go for more information. Your goal should be for the recipients to immediately respond to your letter in a positive way. The Ultimate Sales Letter by Dan S Kennedy is a great resource to help you with your sales copy.

Make an Impact
Your mail piece must stick out from all the rest. Yours will not be the only piece of direct mail that lands on your prospects' doormat today. The more you can do to catch their attention, peak their curiosity, and urge them to open the packet, the better.

Internet Lead Generation
Like traditional lead generation, this new model is founded on demonstrating expertise and building trusting relationships, the difference is that these goals are accomplished online. While

online marketing will continue to evolve, here is a list of some of the proven lead generation techniques that are working now:

Lead Generating Website

A lead generating website is designed to make it easy for clients to understand your value proposition, to download valuable information and to request an offer. The impact of online lead generation can be very dramatic.

Online Networking

No matter what style of social media interaction you work with (Twitter, LinkedIn, Facebook), your main focus should always be about making the right connections with the right people. Online networking can produce the reputation and referrals associated with traditional business networking. You should expect to get results proportionate with the level of your investment of time and attention.

Webinars

A webinar is the online equivalent of a seminar, workshop or other educational event. It requires registration and you can, therefore, collect basic information on a session's attendees. The key to a successful webinar is to select topics that are of great interest and value to your ideal target client. Over time, attendees come to trust your firm and will be likely to consider you when they have a relevant need.

Video Marketing

Video is everywhere today, and for good reason. It is an ideal marketing medium for businesses. Nothing builds credibility like a visual testimony from a client explaining how you solved their problem. It is almost like automating the referral process and it can be used to present your business and explain your services. In each of these roles, video can play an important lead generating and lead nurturing function.

e-Books

One of the most common online lead generating techniques, e-Books can establish credibility and generate qualified leads. You can offer the e-Book on your website (either available free or behind a registration screen), or you can distribute it through third-party services. e-Books also make great Pay-Per-Click offers. If your e-book goes into great depth on a subject, it can generate a great deal of buzz and help to establish your reputation.

Blogging

A blog allows you to create a wide range of keyword-laden content that can be found in the search engines. It can also draw a lot of qualified prospects to your website (this assumes that you host your blog on your website, which I strongly recommend). You can further promote your blog posts on Twitter, LinkedIn and Facebook.

Online lead generation techniques, combined with more traditional marketing, create a formidable strategy for building preference in the marketplace. Online marketing and traditional marketing make a powerful combination and, if utilised to their full potential, could help to catapult your business into a highly successful enterprise.

 Online lead generation techniques, combined with more traditional marketing, create a formidable strategy for building preference in the marketplace."

What next?

I hope you have found this book enjoyable and thought provoking. You should now have a much clearer understanding of how these common mistakes can be addressed, and feel empowered to use your new skills and resources to create positive results in your business.

Love what you do, be innovative and create something that will make you stand out from the crowd. Lead by listening to your staff and customers and be visible to all. Take the time to identify the areas of your business in need of change and commit to taking action. Be consistent in your approach and success will follow.

I look forward to hearing about the impact these simple solutions presented in this book have had on your business.

To Your Success

Emma

" Life has no limitations, except the ones you make."
- Les Brown

About the author

All my life I have been passionate about helping people and making a difference. Having battled with an eating disorder from a very young age I understand how challenging life can sometimes get, however I am living proof that you can come out the other side a much stronger person. Throughout my working career I have gained experience in a variety of sectors including commercial , local authority, charity, education and government which, has resulted in my ability to adapt quickly and effectively to any given situation to bring about positive change.

After college I visited Australia on a working visa. It was here that my passion for travelling took hold. Experiencing the Sydney Olympics was the catalyst that inspired my decision to go to university to study sport. Since then I have been lucky enough to visit many other countries, experiencing different cultures and meeting an abundance of amazing people. A sabbatical from work took me to volunteer at an orphanage in Chiang Mai, Thailand, a grounding experience that I hold very close to my heart.

At university I became qualified as a Personal Trainer and Studio Instructor. I loved helping people change their lifestyle and watch their transformation unfold. Unlike my school days I was extremely conscientious at university and four years down the line I graduated with First Class Honours degree in BSc Sport, Health, Exercise and Nutrition.

For a number of years I worked in the education and charity sector as a mentor to disadvantaged children and young adults. Here I worked closely with each individual to help them improve their physical and mental health and encourage them to return to education, training or employment. This role was challenging, and at times frustrating however, helping someone society had written off turn their life around, made it all worth while.

Following on from there I became the youngest ever Senior Project Manager for the government department established in light of Jamie Oliver's alarming review of school meals in England. Here I was responsible for a number of multi-million pound projects, including the brand creation and build of 27 School FEAST training centres across England, and collaborated with brands such as Disney, Charlie & Lola and Hollyoaks to help engage children and raise the profile of school meals. I was also able to influence the unit content of a number of National Curriculum qualifications surrounding school food, something which resulted in me being invited to the Houses of Parliament.

From here I made the decision to use my knowledge and passion to launch my own business. The lessons within this book are taught during my Step Up one day workshop, helping others to develop new skills and maximise their potential. I am extremely grateful to be able to do a job that I feel truly passionate about and love watching my clients grow their confidence and their business.

My mission is help others win more customers, make more money and have more free time!

For further information or to see how I could help you in your business, please contact me.

 emmamelhuish

0117 244 3678

emma@emmamelhuish.com
Visit www.emmamelhuish.com

Notes: